FROM A BENE

From a Benediction

OLIVIA BYARD

PETERLOO POETS

First published in 1997
by Peterloo Poets
2 Kelly Gardens, Calstock, Cornwall PL18 9SA, U.K.

© 1997 by Olivia Byard

All rights reserved. No part of this publication may be
reproduced, stored in a retrieval system, or transmitted,
in any form or by any means, electronic, mechanical,
photocopying, recording or otherwise without the prior
permission in writing of the publisher.

A catalogue record for this book is available
from the British Library

ISBN 1-871471-72-9

Printed in Great Britain by
Latimer Trend & Company Ltd, Plymouth

ACKNOWLEDGEMENTS are due to the editors of the following journals and newspapers where some of these poems first appeared: *Acumen, Borderlines, Envoi, Iron, Frogmore Papers, Honest Ulsterman, Lines Review, The Observer, Ore, Outposts, Poetry Quarterly, Pennine Platform, Poetry Ireland Review, Poetry Nottingham, Quadrant* (Australia), *Quarry* (Canada), *Smoke, Staple,* and *Weyfarers Magazine.*

I would like to thank David Julier, Anne Ridler and Alastair Fowler for their support and encouragement during the preparation of this volume.

For Chris

who makes it all possible

Contents

Spring Disease

Bulimic eyes unfocused with greed,
I bolt down tall, green-bearded trees;
blossoms hung like heavy udders
or drifting thick down-stream;
cowslip heads sprinkled with dew, by the ream;
pansies marked like a lover's iris,
a few ghostly butterflies,
distracted bees; holly berries;
long bony fingers dripping with leaves;
rose-buds clenched tight as
new-born babies' fists; bluebells;
unfurling aquilegia-worlds
with moons and milky morning mists;
and all washed down with sky, blue
to bursting and stuffed in whole,
edges hanging out like silver
spittle fish. It's a disgraceful,
private, overdone, feast: —
and then the need to digest it.

Whores in Amsterdam

I could not squeeze past their glass to join them,
even in nightmare, so I held back, shy,
while they sat or prowled, divided by reflections
from the milling crowds. Did they dream
of suburban homes before time could weave lace scars
across their thighs and find them sprawled
in cheap cubicles down dirtier alley ways,
pleading for glances from passing vagrants,
as their elder sisters did? Couldn't they reckon
the future? For now, their bodies proud,
they strutted; ultra-violet picking out in white
each frill of négligé, each curved hip:
like frothy sugar icing on birthday cake.
They seemed not to crave display:
bored as they were by the ogling men,
until one, more brave, was plucked in,
a fish from murky water, and swallowed whole
down the business end where beds gaped anatomically
and toilets waited patiently for tit-bits.
Curtains closed on this finale and we left.
Why did I come, and why return next day
en route to the Oudekerk? Why gaze
at my reflection in empty panes,
stork bundles of laundry, the carpet stains?
Was it to learn the limits of my own dark side,
what, if pressed, I could or could not, do?
Or even hide?

At Ruffignac

Deep in the dark's den, past bear-pits
where the grunting and scraping of beasts
hangs palpable, a dried bouquet of sound,
they crawl out to the far edge where ceiling
kneels towards ground, like a mother
to her crying child, and they draw.

A bison, birds, reindeer, sprawl
in cat's graffiti cradle over the cool rock.
Mammoths follow in obedient line,
trunk to truncated tail as though they heard
the piper's dance and found it irresistible.

It is a dry cave; every breath draws itself up
to full height and clamours for attention.
Each shifting pebble up the long nave
towards day's peering eye cries out in alarm.

As I shiver, I see them still, slightly stooped,
paint on, with a serious joy. I smell
the lumbering rank beasts wake for spring,
fix dazed eyes on their crude torches, and listen:
for scurrying small things running below,
the steady drip of time passing, the exact moment.

From Benediction

Trapped outside the gloom of my grandfather's
vestibule by tortured slats of coloured glass,
the sun sent in hues, hostages that spun around,
dazed with freedom, dappling wallpaper pattern-men
red and blue. His sideboard and table
were black giants, great feet that bit the floor
with claws, fruit that marched in rows
of martial splendour up each heavy leg,
scrolls that rolled back polished surfaces
to sphinx-like size and quietude. In glass cases,
china dolls froze in dancing poses,
stiff skirts foamy white, with dusty ribbon hems
(I spoke to their painted pink mouths
behind the see-through bars). At five each dawn,
grandfather and I crept down, stealthy fugitives
in stockinged feet, to feast on cornflakes,
treacle and black tea, while he spoke
in broken English, interchangeably, of treasure
and language. He retrieved handkerchiefs,
shells from linen beaches, to be starched
and ironed carefully; unearthed in folded hoards
after his death. I remember the slash
of pebble dash, sharp, against my finger skin;
pearly soft pink shards half-buried in cement;
too tight to prise loose, as I attended his emergence
from the privy tardis he haunted each night: —
before we tackled hoards of killer weeds
and caught wild strawberries, succulent, for tea.
While he slept, his disembodied teeth snapped,
if he were cross, in their cut-glass jar.
More frequently they smiled: a Cheshire cat's grin,
gleaming white and slightly yellow.

Without Blessing

Tucked up in Aunt Audrey's bed,
talk buzzing around the further rooms
like flies on a hot summer's night,
I watched the door, ajar, and a shaft
of light spread fingers into the room
parting the dark. On one side of the divide
the wardrobe stood stiffly against the wall,
columns and frills on its dark front
not unlike a formal evening shirt.
On the other, my sister and myself,
aboard the bed, flat like a huge raft
above the precipitate fall to carpet;
she, healthily sprawled asleep, a young animal
abandoned to warmth, me, watchful;
alert as the mirror that confronted me
across the lit gulf, a dark opponent
blinking when shadows faltered,
regrouped on passing draughts of air.
I dreamed up stratagems for escape,
to join the razzle-dazzle beyond the door,
but the room's icy chill forbade,
a clammy hand, which shoved me back hard
behind the warm prow of blanket;
while memory intoned that flight
would be futile, an ignominious return
certain and swift. So I lay on guard,
watching shadow battalions manoeuvre
across the ceiling; waited for the furniture
to make the first move; menaced.

A Woman Called Mary

1. ANNUNCIATION

Messengers with wings were superfluous:
I already knew. In dreams I'd held him

on my draped knee. My hand curved over
my belly, pleased; he'd soon be here.

We'd been loving some time in the grove,
trying to forget the heat, the choking dust,

cooled by the quiet flow of our affections;
for it was not passion that joined us,

or need, but a common wish;
awareness of a common cost. It was

my choice as well as his. I knew I'd
witness his death one day, that artefact

of his own design, yet such was my greed,
I smiled for that windpile of hours

in between, the wild harvest, unique
by-product of our love. A weapon to be

honed sharp against the whetstone of
my affections, a cutting edge. Curled, fine,

a small ear inside me now, learning
the knot, the arms that hold, the tree.

2. INTERRUPTED JOURNEY

The jolting was too much for her
and twice they stopped while she retched.
Silence stretched ahead: as though
they swam into it, eerie echoes muffled
by breeze-tides. Stars, not a star lit the way.

The pains began at dawn and he found
shelter. She was racked for hours,
torn by waves of it, until the child
broke the banks of her with head;
on a flood of arms, legs, swam into air.

Her dreams grew big as griffin's wings,
flew around the shabby roof-tops,
until the man with myrrh arrived.
The baby whimpered and the moment ebbed;
she felt her milk flow in; cried.

3. On the Third Day

Part of her would never forgive him
for coming back. She had feared
that nether world he'd wooed and won;
now, tears done, she tended the ground,
pressed holes to harbour new seed.
And as she poured libations into
open-mouthed drills, felt the balm
of detachment, as though life
carried on elsewhere and she,
merely a bridge to it.

Then scarred, honed, he stood there
and she was annoyed: dragged back
to a flickering tallowed half-glow.
She admired the man, watched others
crowd in to touch his hands.
But in time she avoided the circus sounds
to walk fields alone; mourn.
And he must watch her go.

4. ASSUMPTION

Washing dangling, costumes from a play
when the lead has left, will turn grey
by afternoon in the dust and, flapping,
haunt scrawny birds that peck and scratch
the yard's length. A widow with no son
is poor in spite of gifts. She sags
against a wall, deflates with cough;
has coughed all night, a harsh dry sound
like marsh grass. Her fingers run
round well-worn wooden contours, knead
them gently. The time has arrived.

She locks the door when she leaves;
no one finds the key. 'Disappeared into air'
they say, or 'on a cloud'. From one eternity
to another; dust settles like a shroud.

The Child Inside

You sleep; your silence has knives,
your absence lingers. I am used
to your cries, like birds.

I cannot tell if you dream.
Magic words hunch their backs against me.
Doors slam shut.

Again I sit on a doorstep, banging,
rampant to be let in. My din
brings out a raised fist.

Impatient, I wait for you to stir,
rise, run down some charmed path.
Did you die when I was not heeding?

I have seen too many small coffins,
shed tempests of tears. I shake you,
hungry for your breathing.

The Ladybird

(for Susan)

I found her under a rock, damp still
from the husk of the grub she had been.

A small queen, she unfurled, preened,
her large black spots, her glossiness.

We shared delight in the variance of dance,
I touched her wing tips with my own,

then sent her home: to corn, neck bared
for the harvester's chill breeze.

While cold, I saw in memory's stern eye,
the black stubble burning, the fiery sky.

Felt Change

Catching a glimpse of the day before
You died, is like spying a rare bird
Hover in the warm air before its plummet
Down the thermal streams. It can be seen
Just, from afar, as a speck.

You walked in, unaware, as we all are,
Which precise day would be your last,
And we talked a little, of this and that.

And that was that.

At first, your smell lingered on clothes
Crying out for your missing body
Like a mother for a wandering child.

Yet as yesterday receded further,
Shunted along by today's concerns,
Silence took possession
Where your voice had been, until
Cobwebs draped our last conversation.

Girls On the Gower

The coarse ground lent us rough rest
until a blind calf stumbled into our crude tent
laying it flat with a single blow. We emerged;
citizens after war: soaked, bedraggled,
to watch breath rise from the herd
into a grey dawn like smoke from crowds
of coal-fired chimneys. In the low barn
animals warmed us. Shifting uneasily
at our attempts to milk them, cattle were ladies
dancing slowly to entice the reluctant sun.
Collies lounged in the doorway, laughing;
sardonic timekeepers of this gymnastic event,
their quick wits worked the cows like clockwork,
striking time, place, in each slow day
with tiny nudges, wide grins. Their ancestry
was doubtful, but they, supreme; confident
of an elite carved from ability, not pedigree.
Afternoon; donkeys struck across the sands
to Llanelli laden with cockles; women after:
barefoot, prodding the beach with long sticks
and toes. Sweaters clung damply with grim affection
but little success; goose-pimples grew strong
and ambitious. We dreamed of body hair.
Farmers, like our forebears, for this one week,
we followed the blind calf and hungry puppies
doggedly down to the night's dry stabling.

Unfinished Pietà by Michelangelo

Leaning against his mother's cheek,
He could be asleep, except that death
Has dragged his long limbs down.

She holds him in their old embrace,
Moves to kiss his cooling face.
Her tears have not yet formed.

If stone allowed it she would rock him,
Soothe him as she used when he was small,
And he sought comfort for his hurts.

Her grief is waiting in the wings:
A future to make a mother cringe,
Taking form behind her closed eyes.

It is her last chance to support him,
Another moment to hold. If stone let go
Of his lifeless corpse, she would weep.

Donatello's Magdalene

The ideal has fled from you, vanquished;
Left you staring into time's cold face,
Naked except for your hair's cloak.
An outcast, haggard and thin: for you
No bells will ring, no fatted calf
Fear the hiss of the cutting edge.

Refugee from another time, your eyes
Forced wide by horrors they have seen,
Your mouth's bruised hole battered
By harsh sounds: your thin feet
Form lean prints down your marked path.
When will your bitter tears fall?

Uncovering Arezzo — a Meditation

The Tuscan pink stone tower rose
A many-eyed lengthy creature,
High above the stepped street,
Down which the March wind whistled.

Inside, in the crypt, bones were piled.
Like sand settled in an hourglass,
They rose to peaks: the brittle debris
Of a carnivore's lip-smacking meal.

Somehow they shouted of secrets, hissed
Like toothless gossips of sinister death.
How had they been undressed,
These details of saints' lost lives?

We were here for the famous frescoes,
Pilgrims carried by a clattering train,
Through early spring in the Tuscan hills
Where high snow rose over blossom

Like noble brows. This was uncovering
The white life beneath stones. The fat
Eyeless grubs that breathe in the dark
Had fed here on these attenuated Saints.

We had worshipped at our own shrine,
Aided by English language explanations;
Sheba's head saluting Solomon
A living relic of creative life.

But these bones made their claims too,
In the exposed underbelly of Arezzo;
Waiting in glass cases for eternity's
Long chime, eloquent of the skull beneath.

Judas Before Dawn

I thought he had answers, which mattered
to me. So did he, but he seemed

indestructible, like a stout stone
bridge. I didn't know he could

bleed so freely, scream. He lied
when he said he was God. God would

have done it differently, cancelled pain;
this was a man: untidy, like me.

But now, hours won't budge to allow
me to pass, day denies me access

with bloody single-mindedness; sameness
lies strewn across my path, like straw.

I'll dangle this noose, to shake myself
loose of his absence, this awful gain.

Magdalene

My nature haunts you; it wrecks
your peace and leaves you grieving.

For you could never see where I went
while you attended the heavens;

you didn't see me on that further hill
among clouds, speaking with the stars and silence.

Because I serviced men's needs for
my daily bread, you believed that was

my ordained place, although you granted me
your affections. But men who honour not

the tart, get no closer to me
than the wrong key jammed in a locked door,

blocking with pride their only peephole.
Search for where I reside in you

and you'll find yourself anointing
my aching feet. For man, you need time

to untangle your own long hair,
and in time a further miracle, your own tears.

Lazarus Rising

Bandages unravel round my eyes. They flap
Beside me: gulls with broken wings.
Daylight, a bright rectangle outside
This cave, where distant people scurry
Like insect hordes about known tasks.
They ignore me; do not know I rise
In an unstoppable tide. I am invisible
To them: someone to mourn today and leave behind
As life presses on past leavetaking.
My arms now free, I raise a thin hand:
Pull away shroud remnants from my mouth
Like cobwebs. I want to shout, but sound
Staggers at my throat's weak push,
And I croak a whisper. Suddenly, an urgent must
To escape, before that beacon of light
Is snuffed out by some thoughtless tidy hand.
I tear away each cold remaining stone
That secludes me from day, and lurch forward,
A great weight spilling out towards the sun.
A trickle of wet on my still cool cheek,
And warmth are my reward. A first act again,
To lie prone on earth's belly and weep.

Near the Glasshouses

Like stale tea this water stands, staining
its banks with tannin; flies buzz and settle.
Small rocks plop in and drop to the bottom.

She peers. There's movement in the murk. A fish?
A monster fish waiting to snap at carelessly
dipping fingers. Something with no eyes at all?

She withdraws her hand, lingers. Pulls at grass
and scatters it; fishfood. It lies along the lid
like lashes but the surface doesn't blink.

Pond-skaters slide across, slip, collide in heaps:
leggy dirt collecting in immobile corners.
This is a dead eye, a fish eye staring.

She turns to leave tossing a last rock that
briefly disturbs the pond. Hears baleful
movement, but when she turns again, it's gone.

Lilith

She could not submit, had she wished to;
those straddled limbs felt like bars

and she slid through them. Out in the desert,
where sand meets dark in a clash of arms,

dreams slip through her hands, salamanders
enveloped by gritty night. Alone,

no mate to ease down hard spine ridges
which uncurl from a hissing coil, she prays

perfection will sustain with each new game
she plays, but it never does. Sameness clings

limpet to the rock of each experience
the ebb-tide leaves exposed. She hunts appetite.

On Her Easel

The sky stretched tight, held taut
by silver pins of light, she begins.
Slaps a crow in, hunched black and stark
over a post, prey-watching. Unblinking.
But when a slippery paint-worm of wet
oozes out and wriggles, becoming river,
it's spied by crow-eyes and deftly caught.
He gulps his prize and, raucous away,
leaves behind rancour, and an empty canvas day.

Plus Léger Après Bretagne

Stone steps, haphazardly high, rise
to the old daubed door, damp-smelling
wood stacked beside, like soldiers
leaning at ease. I climb up, sit,
and observe the mossy, lichen-clad wall
snake unevenly away towards mistletoe woods.

I am alone: my feet barely brushing
the thick pile of weed-carpeted ground
beneath, while I watch magpies twirl
to raucous cries that penetrate
the corners of this grey spring day
sweeping debris from my tired mind.

I would stay longer, but a fine rain
falls, making my stone seat wet, while
somewhere beyond the trees, sun breaks
the clouds again. I trudge on as before
towards that place, but now, even
in rain, at a steadier, firmer pace.

Intimations

It's as though in all my yesterdays
I were slightly mad, face pressed hard

against experience like glass,
no reflection between it and my flattened nose.

I remember beetles swarming in the night,
their careless slaughter by impassive panes

of a cottage on Lake Huron: our light
a dreadful beacon on a wrecker's beach.

It was my first honeymoon, the years ahead
a magic lantern full of slides, and I refused,

as the carnage increased, to go outside
for fear beetles might die in my hair,

hard carapaces hitting my scalp like hail.
So we stayed, feeling tied, while the evening's

further voice pleaded disarmingly. Next day,
saw driftwood, bloated, at the lake's edge.

Rhossili

I always feared if I dared too near the edge,
I'd plummet down the massive sides of cliff
to lie shattered, and the puzzled sea
would nuzzle my still cheek. But I gambled:
greedy for the line of bay, and the farmhouse,
perched midway along, a lone flower
on the hill's turned brim. A gruelling climb,
but we endured it as penance for indulgence:
to carve imprecations to the gods in sand;
to invade quiet pools stealing gems
that faded to pastiche as they dried;
to huddle in caves below the cliff's huge knees
watching foam tumble, deliciously aware
of submergence at high tide, and fish
swirling past our erstwhile seats.
It was a vessel for mystery; ancient tales:
the Worm's Head held to the land's prow, just,
by one rocky strap. I railed when a road
was born to drag the world's baggage closer,
preferring lost dreams left; that the thirsty tide
lap through all fragile messages.
But inexorable, the road crawled out.

Soliloquy for Early Evening

If I could follow him down
empty streets, stepped and narrow
to the pier, might I shade my eyes
sailor fashion, and watch him paddle,
sun's benediction in his hair,
among the lesser waves.

Should I then sing the so-called siren's song
or leave him be, never say
my chat was cheering the moment on
but he did not speak to that moment
so it fled in haste.

Pull the claws out, pull them out.

Could I once again reiterate
that Hamlet was a noble bore
his girl an only fool and that we're all
attendant lords in our best plays.

It's time to breast the waves.

Could I then take him firmly by the hand,
say I see you've changed your clothes again
how nice, and please come back,
come back for more tea, now.

But what if he prefers to knot
a kerchief for his brow,
and potter near rock pools
searching for collectibles?
What price rebuke?

The claws, the claws, take the claws out!

He's squinting his eyes,
but he's heard, see
the herons beat their wings grandly.

Breasting the waves, breasting.

Scottish Quartet

1. ABOVE GARVE

Urgent, the water tumbles, down, foaming,
clear as insight, over rocks heaved
like heavy hammers and abandoned
to black ground. It's a single composite sound,
save only the lone counterpoint of a sheep
making mutton on this moonscape and bleating
to its rangy lamb. Buzzards swoop and soar
like fast-moving specks in eyes. Arms akimbo,
the valley grieves for her departed, offspring
long gone from the stone croft markers
beside the icy burn. Betrayed to greener pastures,
she yet turns a furrowed brow and gazes
with clear-eyed wonder on these intruders
bumbling rainsuited in an alien space.

2. HIGHLAND HOTEL

A large stag's head stares glassily down,
and one wonders about mice from the dim recesses
of a chintz arm-chair, while doubtfully observing
Miss Fessy's Trout, caught in 1922, and now
balefully behind glass. The fire is lit
in a brave attempt to keep out the damp
and spits spitefully at the rustling
copies of the Telegraph. Fire-dogs loom.
Eyes slide past the Victorian beast
held forever at bay on the vestibule wall
(the original lives with the distiller in London),
round the ornate memorabilia from the Scottish Raj,
(sepia photographs of a royal hunting trip,
two yellowed horns, an open half-hunter,
and some fruit-encrusted porcelain), then wince away
from the sheets being chucked down outside
with business-like intensity by
the determined gods of this place. Possibly
behind all that water there are mountains
to see; but here there's silver service
for haggis and neaps, hot bakewell tart
and lashings of tea. Unfolding an outsize napkin,
feet surreptitiously curled under me, I surrender
to the authenticity of this set-piece oasis.

3. LOCH AILSH

That rock focuses a lax attention,
lacy with lichen, left luggage
on this shore; its edges lapped by water.
To the big music on the pipes,
notes rippling quickly like water
over rocks, small constant changes
accumulating to one sound, deeper
yet grander than its modest beginnings
as a burn in far hills, burbling
and babbling of the heathers and the clouds.
Yet the rock needs another ice-age,
a cataclysm to move.

4. NORTH OF ULLAPOOL

Up to my knees in peat and the hill's
heather skirt, catching gulped cries
from the diving gulls as they crash
the thin air; leaning towards the isles
across rocks long forced askew
by those same huge hands who hold me here,
mute, helpless in my need to slip the line
slide slowly down the strata and veer,
majestic on a stiff breeze, towards
those bright lands shining west of me.
Yanked seared and torn from the rim,
turning sightlessly back. And in.

November Ceasefire

Skeletal trees scarved with thick silence;
a lone dog barks a sharp salute.

Dead leaves wait limp in trenches,
to be swept into the year's mass graves.

Autumn retreats, unveiling beneath
its bright camouflage, a pallid face.

Leaves not killed cleanly by frost
hang limp over poles, in awful example.

Starling scavengers straggle past;
peck at the leaves' empty sockets.

Beneath bushes, dwarf green shoots lurk.
In time they may annex this ravaged place.

Compass

'Wee are made such by love'
— John Donne

When I got up this morning,
I knew you had too,
and the day grew, stretched
and strolled on long legs,
right down the sky's path
to touch the sun's very edge.

When I lay down this evening,
I knew you did too,
and the day died
and left me grieving,
out, out on the world's ledge
where the pale moon loitered too.

Magpie Musical

This solitary character does
his soft-shoe shuffle down
the open road, eye shafting.
He's sleek, in black and white.

I ask after his wife, but
get no reply as he vaults
urbanely onto the verge,
deigns a slight bow.

She's hiding in a hedge
like a shy starlet, betrayed
to my worried eye, just, by
embellishment of dress.

But when they fly, it's worth
the wait. This bachelor and
his occasional mate take to
the air like Astaire and Rogers.

In a single frame they soar,
up and down the cloudless
halls of dance, beating out
joy, fragile joy, together.

Rievaulx Abbey

Arches, swooping deep to the
morning's waist, were a sight,
in quiet dress, grey, edged
with a ribbon of breeze.

I saw cloud vaults there and
light leap mullions. Doves played
arpeggios low and spring
limbered, began to move.

Like insects we swarmed that world,
great legs feeling contours;
parlours, sinks, floors,
were caught like flies in our web

which we stored, until we tired.
Then I found a dead bird in a drain
and we left, for the soaring
spaces had vanished again.

In Vermont at Twelve

Hills flame. As far as the eye skitters,
they are fiery. She pirouettes, skips,

enduring the rasp as her new crinoline
flares in pleasure beneath her skirt,

its hem not unlike smoke that wreathes
experimental loops around her mouth. On the edge

of annual destruction the woods teeter,
burst into a frenzied finale; as though

exhausting themselves of summer heat
before their afterlife as winter wraiths.

She scatters waxy leaves in ruddy torrents,
sticks that crack, snap, like rifle shots;

to her, they herald a huntsman prince,
out of the fairy tale searching for a bride.

Her thoughts blush, hide from him; horizons
gape vermilion, engulf her pilgrim eye.

Scotland in an Oxford Landscape

The stream's tidy banks have fled,
routed, when the river took the borderland
and lost its own identity. Isolated trees
mark mere possibilities, as if this were
a medieval map, where stained brown outlines
suggest the edge of a world which has been
heard of but not yet visited. Dabchicks
drift nodding on the current between,
as though the trunks were supports
for toppled dolmens and they sounded ley lines
like diviners. Beneath, lies debris:
the small river animals' habitats, voles,
otters, rats, avenues of spring anemones,
and tiny wild crocuses that smudge your eyesight
briefly, with enigmatic purple. Treasure,
to be found again, of a more bucolic Atlantis.

December Garden

Sprigs of honesty, angel wings, rustling:
a litter of curling chestnut leaves.

Robin orange breast, a hearth of colour:
mistletoe hats perched on tree-top stands.

A hem of scarlet from summer's fancy robe, trailing:
the spiky punk hair-do of holly.

Moon's large eye in the opaque sky:
an early star, a lover's smile, returning.

A child's toy, a sharp thorn, placed and waiting.

Talking Head

Margaret's face rises from her oyster shroud,
like a sacrifice, a head on a pewter plate.
She is absorbed in death's web of secrets
and ignores me; hints of strange, exotic truths.
Each manicured nail is expressive of piety,
a quality she abhorred in life but her keepers
feel is appropriate to the start of death.
I would clench them into fists,
or at least make them wave, but they look
too brittle, as though they might break,
like bird's wings, so I leave them clipped
and quiescent. She has often been as quiet,
but never this contained; her shroud medieval
and her brow so cold and still, a bird
could sit on it to bathe. I am used to atmosphere,
which she emanated like pungent cooking smells
in friendly kitchens. It is this lack
that is unnerving. She is near
but as a large shell, here to trumpet my loss
and puzzle me; for clarion notes of memory
jar my ears, of where she was, might yet be.

A Walk With Fear

I think of the day when I won't be here,
with bounding sick fear that
I won't be here. Leaves harangue

the air with harsh sounds and there's
blight everywhere: white mould accosts
branches as they snake back towards

silent trunks. I'm trying to see
the earth after me, a muffled, deaf,
sort of invalid world, limping sadly

as we part company; I want to tear
out its crutch so it begs me to stay,
to lift it laughing from the ample ground.

Then I find a tangled garden
to explore in gentle rain. Sick fear,
a well-trained pet, waits patiently.

The Antechamber

Through the half-open door, the tomb,
large in the candle-gloom, my carvings
strewn around the sarcophagus like
sand-worms on a beach. Sealed jars
stand on shelves, mute about their contents.

There are cats, silent and straight,
the occasional dog, wrapped with
meticulous care, and treasure: in piles
on the floor it nauseates like a
too rich meal with its metallic plenitude.

And me, sealed here with my tools and
memories; half-closed doors in my head
leading back down corridors towards
fleeting day; sun's rays after night
has set and sprung its lethal trap.

Hooded Grief

More settled now, it rests on my wrist.
I watch its quick heart beat, wince

only when sharp talons shift tight grip.
Duty to your memory grants me some relief;

unseen, you are with me by your grave,
where I prune a sturdy memorial rose.

While weeks skim past I can leave you there
untended even by thought; a black fleck

hovering nearby. An empty anniversary:
great wings furl; another painful strike.

Sanity's Last Stand

From my eye's corner, hypnotised I stare,
at window frames, and between, like flickers
on the poor screen, shadows scurrying outside
like giant insects. They come from their nests
in waves, darker than night, faster than the eye
can catch; pouring across sight, a black stain.
I check the door as they pile up outside,
sandbag bodies pressing the outside in;
make fervent incantations to the hearth's
dead spider, futile offerings. Then wait,
with that awful sense of nearly seeing,
memory nudged into being but not quite
shoved into words. Until dawn coughs
and splutters, revving its motor; dispersing
the besiegers with exhaust of icy light.
Ambulancemen, quietly, arrive soon after.

Laying Ghosts

I walked back down to Lucy's grave,
fearing decay. The same bird called
again as I approached.

But nature was still kind to her;
The slender mound curved gently to grass,
faded flowers holding close.

She had blended into autumn,
begun to belong. And blown leaves,
bird song, befriend.

Terra Firma

We walk on eggshells, surprised
When they break, sliver into myriad
Pieces beneath unwary feet.

Just below the stout stone tower
Lies molten rock, ready to churn
When a thousand ages stop.

See buildings topple; see people quake.
Yesterday, just there, were cafés,
Pigeons eating bread crumbs.

Today we huddle and hide
From blows that strike us like weather.
Eyes in hollow sockets struck dumb.

Flags

Again the iris came, but this year
we missed them. Frost burned buds lured out
by early spring's warm words.

They hung limp, grey on stems:
wrinkled french letters; blue flags
with strange yellow eyes that never opened.

But seas of bluebells showed, shimmering.
Heat rose, palpable, as though this were
Provence and Monet sat down to paint.

You sat there too: red shorts, bare feet,
bright bunting on the day's tall masts,
watching with me, the regatta sail.

We steered apart at half-mast after.

A Child Leaves Home

(for Mike)

I grieve for your dead childhood:
abandoned, an empty casing, a chrysalis.
A few of your things remain, too trivial
or precious for your maiden flight,
and, talismen in safe hidey-holes,
I squirrel them away: while they stay,
you must return. After we left you,
your wings folded quietly by your sides,
looking forlorn, almost untried, I cried
for your fragility. That capsule of time
encases me still, a hard case from which
I will only crack free when you return;
and I admire your wing-span.

The Disappearance

Dawdling in the classroom, commotion
coming on a bore-tide, we spied

her desk exposed and empty. They pulled
the blinds so we must guess the mess

the bus had made of her, left us
captive to our young imaginations.

We saw the double decker mounting,
squeezing out life in its excitement;

squashing her thoughtlessly, an insect
underfoot; pictured smears of crushed brain,

guts spilling across tarmac; rushed to exclaim
when escape bells finally clanged.

All traces of accident had been removed.
Her desk waited patiently until term's end.

Theft

Her childhood was thieved, not at night
when terrors beat wings, but while the sun
reared helpless against window panes
before falling hard from the sky's arms.
Since then she has mourned in a twilight
that lurks to catch dark.

The whole thing reminds her of rings
on men's fingers: tight rings that scratch
flesh, like chalk across a blackboard.
Even the memory of her own reflection
jars with its companion glass of
dentists' drills, blood in baths.

His legs were everywhere; his touch
a careless sting; she knows
she should no longer cringe, but,
helpless, screams at smallish spiders
that crawl on grubby porcelain. An old
thief stole her youth, junked it afterward.

Shapechanger

Froth on a celestial drink, frogspawn
Thick across the pond. Weed hairs
Flow up from roots; a woman submerged beyond.
We cannot see through the murk
Find her, without gills.
Held in air's tight rills, we only
Dream of her steps through dark fronds.

I too would hide, dart deep to where
My own dreams flow, my swirling hair
Stirred by eddies in the currents above;
Then protected from all peering eyes,
Golden feet begin to move.

Beyond Farewell

The house rattles emptiness at me,
Even its ghosts are absent.
I pack myself with activity:
The shouts of my pots and pans quell
Absence for a while, but, stolid,
Refusing to be cowed, it stirs again.

Memories of celebration echo loudly,
Ricochet. When you left, chairs
Were tipped over; candles snuffed.
I drift through the debris, hoping to hear
One voice say, play it.
But the stubborn piano stays silent.

Getting the Wind Up

Shadow-men in frock coats long behind,
shutting the dark softly with gloved hands,
I and my Baskerville hound push
onto this stage of hush. The moon's
gone off, to mope perhaps, in her dressing-room
and there's only the sky-drop left,
billowing black, tulle tucked with pins
that cast no light past the arc
around me. Front of house, pitch, thick
with eyes that glow, mouths that sigh,
and the rustling. Hairs on end, I'm poised
here attending the coward's prompt.